Cont

The year indicated beside each of th　　　　　　　　　　　　)f
this type first appear in the Framewoi　　　　　　　　　　　lt
does not mean that all the words incl　　　　　　　　　　　t
in that year.

Section A. High and medium frequency words (lists 1 and 2)

1. Reception
2. Year 1 and Year 2
3. Year 4 and Year 5

Section B. Phonic knowledge (includes list 3)

1. CVCs (R/Y1)
2. Consonant clusters (R)
3. Word endings ck/ff/ll/ss/ng (Y1 T2)
4. Initial consonant clusters (Y1 T2)
5. End consonant clusters (Y1 T2)
6. Long vowel phonemes (Y1 T3)
7. Short vowel phonemes (Y2 T1)
8. Vowel phonemes 'air','or','er' (Y2 T2)
9. Vowel phonemes 'ear','ea' (Y2T3)
10. Other digraphs (Y2)
11. Multi-syllabic words (Y2)

Section C. Spelling conventions and rules

1. Prefixes (Y3)
2. Suffixes (Y3)
3. Words ending in '–le' (Y3)
4. Silent letters (Y3)
5. Compound words (Y3)
6. Two syllable words with double consonants (Y4)
7. Suffixes (Y4)
8. Common endings (Y4)
10. Vowel endings other than 'e' (Y5)
11. Prefixes (Y5)
12. Suffixes (Y5)
13. Prefixes (Y6)

Section A. High and medium frequency words (lists 1 and 2)

The National Literacy Strategy Framework for Teaching provides a list of high frequency words divided into two parts. The first part consists of 45 words which children are expected to encounter in Reception. These words should be reinforced in Years 1 and 2.

The second part of list 1 gives a further 113 words – plus the days of the week, months of the year, numbers to twenty and common colours – which children should cover by the end of Year 2.

A1. Reception

a	like
all	look
am	me
and	mum
are	my
at	
away	no
big	of
	on
can	
cat	play
come	said
dad	see
day	she
dog	
for	the
	they
get	this
go	to
going	up
he	was
	we
I	went
in	
is	yes
it	you

A2. Year 1 and Year 2

about	first
after	from
again	girl
an	good
another	got
as	
back	had
ball	half
be	has
because	have
bed	help
been	her
boy	here
brother	him
but	his
by	home
	house
call	how
called	
came	if
can't	
could	jump
	just
did	last
do	laugh
don't	little
dig	live
door	lived
down	love

A2. Year 1 and Year 2 (cont)

love
made
make
man
many
may
more
much
must

name
new
next
night
not
now

off
old
once
one
or
our
out
over

people
push
pull
put

ran

saw
school
seen
should

sister
so
some

take
than
that
their
them
then
there
these
three
time
too
took
tree
two

us

very

want
water
way
were
what
when
where
who
will
with
would

your

plus the days of the week, months of the year, numbers to twenty and common colours.

Sunday	six
Monday	seven
Tuesday	eight
Wednesday	nine
Thursday	ten
Friday	eleven
Saturday	twelve
	thirteen
January	fourteen
February	fifteen
March	sixteen
April	seventeen
May	eighteen
June	nineteen
July	twenty
August	
September	black
October	blue
November	brown
December	green
	orange
zero	purple
one	red
two	yellow
three	white
four	
five	

A3. Year 4 and Year 5

*Year 3 is for consolidation of the word lists from Key Stage 1. The Framework gives a further list for Key Stage 2, this time of **medium frequency words** (list 2). These words are for Year 4 and the first two terms of Year 5. The final term of Year 5 and all Year 6 are for consolidation of the word lists covered earlier in Key Stage 2.*

above
across
almost
along
also
always
animals
any
around
asked
baby
balloon
before
began
being
below
better
between
birthday
both
brother
brought
can't
change
children
clothes
coming
didn't
different
does
don't
during

earth
every
eyes
father
first
follow
following
found
friends
garden
goes
gone
great
half
happy
head
heard
high
I'm
important
inside
jumped
knew
know
lady
leave
light
might
money
morning
mother

mother
much
near
never
number
often
only
opened
other
outside
own
paper
place
right
round
second
show
sister
small
something
sometimes
sound
started
still
stopped
such
suddenly
sure
swimming
think
those

thought
through
today
together
told
tries
turn
turned
under
until
upon
used
walk
walked
walking
watch
where
while
white
whole
why
window
without
woke
woken
word
work
world
write
year
young

Section B. Phonic knowledge (includes list 3)

*List 3 in The Framework consists of specific phonics and spellings for R to Year 2. It covers simple vowel sounds, consonant clusters, more difficult phonemes, and spelling patterns of increasing complexity. We have compiled a list of most of the words children will encounter which feature the phonemes and letter combinations given in list 3. We have grouped these according to the years in which The Framework states they should be first taught. **Please note that we do not suggest that all the words we give are suitable for the first year to which they are attached.** The year indicated is only the starting point for the introduction of the particular phonemes and letter combinations. Many of the words in our lists will be more suitable for consolidation at a later stage.*

B1. (CVC) combinations
(R and Year 1)

bad	cog	fun	hot
bag	cop	gag	hub
ban	cot	gap	hug
bat	cub	gel	hum
bed	cup	gem	hut
beg	cut	get	jab
bet	dab	god	jam
bib	dad	got	jet
bid	dam	gum	jig
big	den	gun	job
bin	did	gut	jog
bit	dig	had	jot
	dim	hag	jug
	din	ham	lad
bog	dip	has	lap
bud	dog	hat	led
bug	dot	hem	leg
bun	dug	hen	let
bus	fan	him	lid
but	fat	hip	lip
cab	fib	hit	lit
can	fig	hob	log
cap	fin	hod	lot
cat	fit	hog	
cod	fog	hop	

continued over ☞

B1. (CVC) combinations
(R and Y1) (cont.)

mad	pub	tat	wet
mam	pun	ten	wig
man	pup	tin	win
map	put	tip	wit
mat	rag	top	won
men	ram	tot	yam
met	ran	tub	yap
mob	rap	tug	yes
mop	rat	van	yet
mud	red	vet	zap
mug	rib	wag	zig-zag
mum	rid	web	zip
nag	rig	wed	
nan	rim		
nap	rip		
net	rob		
nib	rod		
nil	rot		
nip	rub		
nod	rug		
not	rum		
nut	run		
pad	rut		
pal	sad		
pan	sag		
pat	sap		
peg	sat		
pen	set		
pet	sip		
pig	sit		
pin	sob		
pip	sum		
pit	sun		
pod	tag		
pop	tan		
pot	tap		

B2. Consonant clusters ch, sh and th (R)

*The Framework indicates that children in Reception classes should, in addition to initial consonants and short vowel sounds, learn to recognise **ch**, **sh** and **th**. Many of the words beginning with these phonemes which children will encounter and use (although probably not yet read or write) are listed below.*

ch–
chain
chair
chalk
chamber
champ
champion
chance
change
chapter
charge
chariot
charm
charming
chart
chat
chatter
cheap
cheat
check
cheer
cheerful
cheese
cherry
chest
chestnut
chicken
child
children
chill
chimney
chimpanzee

chin
chip
chocolate
choice
choose
chop
chopsticks
chunk
church
sh–
shabby
shack
shadow
shaft
shake
shall
shallow
shame
shampoo
shan't
shape
share
shark
sharp
sharpen
shatter
shawl
shave
sheaf
shear
sheath
shed

sheep
sheet
shelf
shell
shelter
shepherd
sherbet
shin
shine
ship
shirt
shiver
shock
shoe
shop
shopping
short
shorten
shorts
show
should
shoulder
shower

th–
than
thank
that
thatch
thaw
theatre
them
theme (park)

themselves
then
there
thermometer
thief
their
thigh
thin
think
thing
thirsty
this
thistle
thorn
thorough
thoroughly
thought
thousand
thrash
thread
threat
threaten
three
threw
through
throw
thud
thumb
thump
thunder
Thursday

B3. Word endings ck/ff/ll/ss/ng (taught from Y1 T2)

–ck	tack	rack	bill
back	tick	rock	bull
black	tick tock	rucksack	call
brick	track	sack	dell
check	trick	sick	doll
chick	truck	sock	dull
chicken	tuck	stick	fall
click	wick	stuck	fell
clock	wreck	suck	fill
deck		tack	frill
dock	**–ck**	tick	full
duck	back	tick tock	gill
flick	black	track	gull
frock	brick	trick	hall
hack	check	truck	hill
haddock	chick	tuck	kill
haystack	chicken	wick	lull
kick	click	wreck	
knock	clock		mill
lack	deck	**–ff**	pill
lick	dock	cuff	pull
lock	duck	cliff	sill
luck	flick	fluff	sell
mock	frock	gruff	small
muck	hack	huff	smell
pack	haddock	off	stall
peck	haystack	puff	skill
pick	kick	ruff	spell
rack	knock	sniff	spill
rock	lack	staff	still
rucksack	lick	stiff	tall
sack	lock	stuff	tell
sick	luck	whiff	till
sock	mock		wall
stick	muck	**–ll**	well
stuck	pack	all	will
suck	peck	ball	yell
	pick	bell	

B3. Word endings ck/ff/ll/ss/ng (cont)

B4. Initial consonant clusters (taught from Y1 T2)

–ss
boss
class
fuss
guess
hiss
kiss
lass
less
loss
mass
mess
miss
moss
pass
press
toss

–ng
bang
bong
bung
bring
clang
cling
clung
ding
dong
dung
fang
fling
flung
gang
gong
hang
hung
king

long
lung
mung (bean)
pang
ping
pong
prong
rang
ring
rung
sang
sing
sling
song
string
strong
sung
swing
swung
thing
thong
wing
wring
wrung
wrong
zing

plus present participles of regular verbs – e.g. running, walking, smiling, talking, etc.

bl–
black
blackberry
blackbird
blame
blank
blanket
blast-off
bleach
bleed
blend
blender
blind
blink
blister
blood
blossom
blot
blow
blue

br–
bra
brace
bracelet
brain
brake
branch
brand
brave
brawl
bray
breach
bread
break
breakfast
breast

breath
breathe
breeches
breed
breeze
bribe
brick
bride
bridge
bridle
bright
brilliant
brim
bring
brink
broad (bean)
broadcast
broken
bronze
brooch
brood
brook
broom
broomstick
brother
brought
brow
brown
browse
bruise
brung
brush
brute
brutal

continued over ☞

B4. Initial consonant clusters (continued)

cl–
clad
claim
clam
clammy
clamp
clan
clang
clanger
clank
clap
clarinet
clash
clasp
class
classic
classroom
clatter
clause
claw
clay
clean
clear
clerk
clever
click
cliff
climb
cling
clink
clinic
clip
cloak
cloakroom
clock
clod
clog

clone
close
clot
cloth
clothes
cloud
clover
clown
club
cluck
clue
clump
clumsy
cluster
clutch
clutter

cr–
crab
crack
cracker
crackle
cradle
crag
crane
crash
crate
crave
crawl
crayon
crazy
cream
create
creative
creature
creed
creep
credible

crest
crib
cricket
crime
criminal
crimson
crinkle
cringe
crisp
criss-cross
croak
crocodile
crocus
cross
crossword
crow
crown
cruel
crumb
crunch
crust
cry
crystal

dr–
drab
draft
drag
dragon
drain
drake
dram
drama
drank
drape
drastic
draught
draughts

draw
drawl
drawer
drawing
dread
dreadful
dream
dreary
dredge
drench
dress
dresser
dressing
drew
dribble
dried
drier
drift
drill
drink
drip
drive
drizzle
droop
drop
drone
dross
drown
drowsy
drug
drum
dry

B4. Initial consonant clusters (continued)

dw–
dwarf
dwell
dwelling
dwindle

fl–
flabby
flag
flake
flame
flan
flank
flannel
flap
flapjack
flare
flash
flask
flat
flatten
flatter
flavour
flaw
flea
flee
fleece
fleet
flesh
flew
flex
flick
flicker
flight
flimsy
flinch
fling
flint

flip
flit
flipper
float
flock
flog
flood
floor
flop
floss
flour
flow
flower
flu
flue
fluent
fluff
fluke
flush
flute
flutter
fly

fr–
fraction
fracture
fragile
fragment
frail
frame
frank
frantic
fraud
fray
freak
freckle
free
freeze

freezer
freight
frenzy
frequent
fresh
fret
friar
friction
Friday
fridge
friend
fright
frill
fringe
frisk
fritter
frock
frog
from
front
frontier
frost
froth
frown
frozen
fruit
frustrate
fry

gl–
glacier
glad
gladiator
glamour
glance
gland
glare
glass

glasses
glaze
gleam
glee
glide
glimmer
glimpse
glint
glisten
glitter
gloat
global
globe
gloom
glorify
glorious
glory
gloss
glossary
glove
glow
glower
glue
glum

gr–
grab
grace
gracious
grade
gradient
gradual
grain
gram
grammar
grand
grandad

continued over ☞

B4. Initial consonant clusters (continued)

grandchild
grandfather
grandma
grandmother
grandpa
granite
grant
grape
grapefruit
graph
graphic
grasp
grass
grate
grateful
grating
gratitude
grave
gravel
gravity
gravy
graze
grease
great
greed
green
greenery
greet
greeting
grew
grey
grid
grill
grim
grime
grin
grind

grip
grisly
gristle
grit
grizzly bear
groan
grocer
groggy
groin
groom
groove
grope
gross
grotesque
ground
group
grouse
grovel
grow
growl
grub
grubby
grudge
gruesome
gruff
grumble
grumpy
grunt

pl–
place
placid
plague
plaice
plain
plaintive
plait
plan
plane
planet
plank
plant
plantation
plaster
plastic
plat
platform
platinum
platoon
play
playstation
plead
pleasant
please
pleasure
pledge
plenty
pliers
plod
plop
plot
plough
pluck
plug
plum
plumber

plump
plunge
plural

pr–
practical
practice
practise
praise
pram
prance
prank
prawn
pray
prayer
preach
precious
predator
predict
preface
prefect
prefer
prefix
pregnant
prehistoric
prejudice
prelude
premier
premium
prep
prepare
prescribe
prescription
presence
present
presenter
presently
preserve

B4. Initial consonant clusters (continued)

preside	proceeds	proportion	scanner
president	process	propose	scanty
press	procession	proprietor	scapegoat
pressure	prod	prose	scar
prestige	prodigal	prosecute	scarce
pretend	produce	prospect	scare
pretty	product	prosper	scarf
prevent	production	protect	scarlet
preview	profession	protein	scary
prey	professor	protest	scatter
prevent	profile	protractor	scene
prey	profit	protrude	scent
price	profound	proud	sceptical
prick	program	prove	schedule
pride	programme	proverb	scheme
priest	progress	provide	scholar
prim	prohibit	province	school
primary	project	provisions	schooner
primate	projector	provoke	science
prime	prolog	prow	scientist
primer	prolong	prowl	scissors
primitive	prominent	prune	scone
primrose	promise	pry	scoop
prince	promising		scooter
princess	promote	**sc–**	scope
principal	prompt	scab	scorch
principle	prone	scabbard	score
print	prong	scaffold	scorn
priority	pronoun	scaffolding	scorpion
prise	pronounce	scald	Scot
prism	proof	scale	scoundrel
prison	prop	scales	scout
private	prop	scalp	scowl
privilege	propel	scamp	
prize	propeller	scamper	
probable	proper	scampi	
problem	property	scan	
proceed	prophet	scandal	

B4. Initial consonant clusters (continued)

scr–
scramble
scrap
scrape
scrappy
scratch
scrawl
scream
screech
screw
Scrabble
scribble
script
scripture
scroll
scrounge
scrub
scruffy
scrum
scuba (dive)
scuffle
sculptor
sculptures-
cumm
scurry
scuttle

shr–
shred
shrew
schrewd
shriek
shrill
shrimp
shrine
shrink
shrivel
shroud

shrub
shrug
shrunk

sk–
skate
skateboard
skeleton
sketch
skewer
ski
skid
skill
skim
skimp
skin
skint
skip
skipper
skirt
skirting
skit
skittish
skittle
skull
skunk
sky
skydiver
skylight
skyscraper

sl–
slab
slack
slacks
slain
slam
slander
slang

slant
slap
slapstick
slash
slat
slate
slaughter
slave
slay
sledge
sleek
sleep
sleeper
sleet
sleeve
sleigh
slender
slept
slew
slice
slick
slide
slight
slime
slime
sling
slink
slip
slipper
slipshod
slit
slither
sliver
slog
slogan
slop
slope

slosh
slot
sloth
slouch
slovenly
slow
sludge
slug
slum
slumber
slump
slung
slunk
slur
slush
sly

sm–
smack
small
smallpox
smart
smash
smear
smell
smile
smithereens
smock
smog
smoke
smooth
smother
smoulder
smudge
smuggle
smut

B4. Initial consonant clusters (continued)

sn–
snack
snag
snail
snake
snap
snappy
snare
snarl
snatch
sneak
sneer
sneeze
sniff
snigger
snip
snob
snooker
snoop
snooze
snore
snort
snout
snow
snowdrop
snowflake
snowman
snub
snug
snuggle

sp–
space
spade
spaghetti
span
spaniel
spank

spanner
spare
spark
sparkle
sparrow
spat
spatter
spawn
speak
spear
special
species
speck
spectacles
spectator
speech
speed
spell
spend
spice
spider
spike
spill
spin
spindle
spine
spiral
spire
spit
spite
spoil
spoke
sponge
spook
spoon
spool
sport

spot
spout
spud
spun
spur
spurt
spy

spl–
splash
splatter
splendid
splinter
split

spr–
sprain
spray
spread
spreadsheet
spring
sprinkle
sprint
sprout
spruce

squ–
squabble
squad
squall
squander
square
squash
squat
squeak
squeal
squeeze
squelch
squid

squiggle
squint
squirm
squirrel
squirt

st–
stab
stable
stack
stadium
staff
stag
stage
stagger
stain
stair
stake
stale
stalk
stall
stammer
stamp
stampede
stand
standard
standby
standstill
staple
star
starch
stare
starfish
starling
start
starter
startle

continued over ☞

B4. Initial consonant clusters (continued)

starvestate
statement
statesman
static
station
stationary
stationery
statistic
statue
status
stay
steady
steak
steal
stealthy
steam
steed
steel
steep
steeple
steer
stem
stencil
step
stepfather
stepmother
stereo
sterling
stern
stew
steward
stick
sticker
stiff
stifle
stile
still

stilts
sting
stingy
stink
stir
stitch
stoat
stock
stocking
stockpile
stocks
stocky
stodgy
stoke
stole
stomach
stone
stood
stool
stoop
stop
store
storey
stork
storm
story
stout
stove
stow
stub
stubble
stubborn
stuck
stud
student
studio
study

stuff
stuffing
stuffy
stumble
stump
stun
stunt
stupid
sturdy
stutter
sty
style
stylus

str–
staddle
straggle
straight
strain
straits
strand
strange
stranger
strangle
strap
strategy
straw
strawberry
stray
streak
stream
street
strength
strenuous
stress
stretch
stretcher
strew

stricken
strict
stride
strife
strike
striker
string
strip
stripe
strive
strobe
stroke
stroll
strong
struggle
strut

sw–
swagger
swallow
swamp
swan
swank
swap
swarm
swat
sway
swear
sweat
sweatshirt
swede
sweep
sweeper
sweet
swell
swerve
swift
swill

B4. Initial consonant clusters (continued)

swim
swindle
swine
swing
swipe
swirl
swish
switch
swivel
swollen
swoon
swoop
swop
swot

thr–
thrash
thread
threat
three
thresh
threshold
threw
thrift
thrill
thriller
throat
throb
throne
throng
throttle
through
throw
thrush
thrust

tr–
trace
track

tracksuit
traction
tractor
trade
tradition
traffic
tragedy
tragic
trail
trailer
train
trainer
trainers
traitor
tram
tramp
trample
trampoline
trance
transfer
transform
transfusion
transistor
transplant
transport
trap
trapeze
trash
travel
trawler
tray
treacherous
treacle
tread
treason
treasure
treat

treatment
treaty
treble
tree
trek
trellis
tremble
tremor
trench
trend(y)
trespass
trestle
trial
triangle
tribe
tribute
trick
trickle
trifle
trigger
trim
Trinity
trio
trip
tripe
triple
triplet
tripod
triumph
trivial
troll
trolley
trombone
troop
trophy
tropic
trot

trouble
trough
trousers
trout
trowel
truant
truce
truck
trudge
true
trumpet
truncheon
trundle
trunk
trust
truth
try

tw–
tweak
tweed
tweezers
twelve
twenty
twice
twiddle
twig
twilight
twin
twine
twinkle
twirl
twist
twitch
twitter

B5. End consonant clusters (taught from Year 1 Term 2)

–ld
bald
bold
build
cold
could
fold
gild
gold
guild
held
hold
mould
old
should
sold
told
weld
would

–nd
abound
and
aground
around
astound
band
bend
bond
bound
brand
brigand
command
defend
demand
depend
end
end

fend
find
fond
found
frond
fund
ground
hand
kind
land
land
lend
mend
mind
mound
remind
pond
profound
rebound
resound
rind
round
sand
send
sound
spend
stand
strand
surround
tend
wand
wind

–lf
calf
elf
golf
half
self
shelf
wolf

–lth
health
stealth
wealth

–nch
bench
branch
bunch
clench
crunch
drench
finch
flinch
French
hunch
inch
lunch
lynch
munch
ranch
stench
tench
trench
wench
winch
wrench

–lk
chalk
milk
silk
sulk
stalk
talk
walk

–nk
bank
blink
brink
bunk
chink
chunk
clank
clink
drink
honk
hunk
ink
link
junk
monk
pink
rank
rink
sank
sink
skunk
stink
sunk
tank
thank
think
wink
yank

B5. End consonant clusters (continued)

–sk
ask
bask
brisk
cask
desk
disk
dusk
husk
mask
risk
rusk
task
tusk

–lp
alp
gulp
help
pulp
scalp
yelp

–mp
amp
bump
camp
champ
chimp
chomp
clamp
clump
cramp
damp
dump
hemp
hump
imp
jump

lamp
limp
lump
plump
pump
ramp
romp
rump
scamp
slump
stamp
stomp
stump
sump
thumb
tramp
wimp

–sp
clasp
crisp
lisp
wasp
wisp

–ct
act
duct
fact
pact
tact
tract

–ft
daft
drift
left
loft
raft

sift
soft
rift
waft

–lt
assault
belt
bolt
colt
fault
felt
halt
hilt
kilt
melt
moult
quilt
salt
spilt
stilt
tilt

–nt
ant
bent
can't
chant
confident
count
dent
dependent
don't
elephant
flint
font
fount
grant
grunt

hint
hunt
ignorant
independent
infant
jubilant
leant
learnt
lent
lint
meant
mint
mount
pant
pint
plant
pleasant
punt
rant
sent
serpent
shan't
spent
sprint
squint
stint
tent
tint
unpleasant
want
went
won't

continued over ☞

B5. End consonant clusters (continued)

–pt
apt
crept
leapt
kept
slept
wept
wrapt

–st
aghast
arrest
August
best
blast
boast
breast
bust
cast
chest
coast
crest
crust
dust
fast
feast
first
frost
ghost
guest
gust
host
jest
just
last
list
lost
mast

mist
most
must
nest
optimist
past
pessimist
pest
post
quest
rest
roast
rust
test
thirst
thrust
toast
trust
vast
vest
west
worst
wrist

*plus superlatives
such as happiest,
saddest, fastest,
slowest, etc.*

–xt
context
next
text
twixt

B6. Long vowel phonemes (taught from Year 1 Term 3)

i. 'ee' sound

ee
beech
beep
bleep
breed
breeze
creep
deep
feed
feel
feet
fleet
freeze
green
greet
heed
heel
jeep
keel
keen
keep
meet
peel
peep
queen
queer
screech
see
seed
sheep
sheet
sleek
sleep
sleet
speed
steep

steel
steer
street
sweep
sweet
three
tree

ea
beam
beat
clean
cream
dream
each
easel
easy
eat
feat
flea
gleam
grease
heal
heap
heat
jeans
lean
leap
mean
meat
neat
peal
peat
please
pleat
preach

reach
read
real
reap
reason
scream
seal
seat
sneak
squeak
squeal
steal
steam
stream
teacher
treat
tweak
wheat

B6. Long vowel phonemes (taught from Year 1 Term 3)

ii. 'ay' sound

ai	a-e		
afraid	age	pale	pay
again	ape	pane	play
aid	ate	place	portray
aim	blade	plane	pray
braid	blame	plate	ray
brain	cage	race	repay
chain	cake	rage	Saturday
claim	cape	rake	say
drain	cradle	safe	slay
fail	crane	sage	spray
faith	date	sale	stay
frail	drape	same	stray
gain	escape	scrape	Sunday
grain	face	skate	sway
hail	fade	snake	Thursday
jail	fake	space	tray
mail	fame	spade	Tuesday
main	flame	stage	way
nail	frame	stale	Wednesday
pail	gate	tale	
plain	game	trade	
sail	grace	whale	
sailor	grape	**ay**	
Spain	grate	away	
sprain	hate	bay	
stain	lace	bray	
straight	lame	clay	
strain	lane	day	
tail	late	Friday	
trail	made	gay	
trailer	make	hay	
train	male	jay	
	mane	lay	
	name	may	
	pace	Monday	

B6. Long vowel phonemes (continued)

iii. 'igh' sound

ie
die
flies
lie
magpie
pie
tie
untie

i-e
alike
bike
bite
chime
dine
file
fine
hide
hike
kite
like
line
mile
mime
mine
pine
prime
ride
rite
shine
side
site
smile
smite
spike
tide

tile
time
tire
tribe
tripe
trike
vine
white
wine
write

igh
bright
delight
fight
flight
fright
high
knight
light
might
night
right
sigh
sight
thigh
tight

y
by
cry
defy
dry
fly
fry
imply
July

my
nearby
occupy
pry
satisfy
shy

sty
supply
terrify
try
wry

iv. 'oh' sound

oa
boast
boat
charcoal
coal
coast
coat
foal
goal
goat
load
loaf
oaf
oak
oats
moan
moat
road
roast
shoal
stoat
toad
toast

o-e
alone
bone
broke
choke
code

coke
cone
drone
hole
home
joke
lone
mode
mole
note
phone
poke
pole
prone
rode
role
rote
scone
sole
spoke
stoke
stole
stone
tone
tote
vole
vote
whole
woke

B6. Long vowel phonemes (continued)

iv. 'oh' sound (continued)

ow			
arrow	fallow	mellow	sow
bellow	follow	minnow	sparrow
below	flow	mow	swallow
bow	flown	row	throw
blow	furrow	shallow	tomorrow
bowl	grow	show	tow
burrow	hollow	slow	yellow
crow	know	snow	
	low	sorrow	

v. 'oo' sound

oo	u-e	new
baboon	brute	pew
balloon	crude	screw
bamboo	dune	sewer
boot	flute	shrew
broom	June	stew
food	jute	strew
groom	minute	view
harpoon	prune	
loot	tune	**ue**
maroon		avenue
monsoon	**ew**	blue
mood	blew	clue
moon	brew	cruel
noon	chew	cue
salloon	crew	due
scooter	drew	hue
shampoo	ewe	issue
shoot	few	queue
soon	flew	rescue
spoon	grew	sue
swoon	knew	true
	mew	value

B7. Short vowel phonemes (from Year 2 Term 1)

i. 'u' sound

oo	stood	dull	seagull
blood	wood	full	and words
flood	**u**	gull	ending in –ful, e.g.
good	bull	mull	thankful, faithful,
hood	cull	pull	dreadful, etc.

ii. 'ah' sound

ar	cargo	garbage	lark
alarm	carnation	garden	larva
are	carnival	gargle	leopard
arch	carnivore	gargoyle	leotard
arm	carp	garland	margin
art	carpet	garlic	march
artist	carpenter	garment	March
bar	cart	garnish	mark
barb	cartilage	garter	market
barbecue	carton	guard	marsh
barber	cartoon	guardian	martial
bard	cartwheel	hard	Martian
barge	carve	hardly	martyr
bark	char	hardy	marvel
barley	charcoal	hark	monarch
barman	charge	harm	mortar
bar mitzvah	charger	harmonica	parcel
barn	charm	harmony	parched
barnacle	chart	harness	parchment
barter	charter	harp	pardon
car	dark	harpoon	park
carbon	darn	harsh	parka
carcass	dart	harvest	parliament
card	far	jar	parsley
cardboard	farm	larch	parson
cardigan	farther	lard	parsnip
cardinal	farthing	large	

continued over ☞

B7. Short vowel phonemes (continued)

ii. 'ah' sound (continued)

ar (cont.)	scar	spark	superstar
part	scarf	sparkle	tar
partial	scarlet	sparse	target
particle	shark	star	tarmac
parting	sharp	starch	tarnish
partner	smart	stark	tart
party	snarl	start	tartan
radar	spar	starve	varnish

iii. 'oy' sound

oi	oily	**oy**	joy
boil	ointment	alloy	oyster
broil	point	annoy	ploy
coil	poison	boy	royal
coin	recoil	convoy	soya
foil	soil	cowboy	toy
gumboil	spoil	coy	
hydrofoil	tinfoil	decoy	
oil	toil	destroy	
oilfield	toilet	employ	
oilskin	turmoil	employment	

iv. 'n<u>ow</u>' sound

ow	cowboy	gown	scowl
allow	cowslip	how	slowdown
anyhow	crowd	howl	somehow
bow	crown	lowdown	sow
brow	down	now	town
brown	drown	powder	vow
cow	fowl	renown	wow!
coward	frown	row	
ou	compound	hound	rebound
about	count	joust	round
around	doubt	mound	sound
background	fairground	mountain	spellbound
bough	found	pounce	surround
bound	fountain	pound	underground

B8. Vowel phonemes 'air', 'or', 'er' (from Year 2 Term 2)

i. 'air' sound

air	**are**	**ere**
airborne	aware	ampere
aircraft	bare	anywhere
airfield	beware	elsewhere
airlift	blare	nowhere
airline	care	somewhere
airtight	compare	there
affair	dare	where
chair	declare	
dairy	fanfare	**ear**
despair	fare	bear
éclair	flare	overbear
fair	glare	pear
fairy	hare	swear
flair	mare	tear
hair	nightmare	underwear
impair	prepare	wear
lair	rare	
millionaire	scare	
mohair	share	
pair	snare	
pushchair	software	
questionnaire	stare	
repair	square	
solitaire	ware	
stairs	warfare	
wheelchair	welfare	

ii. 'or' sound

or	conductor	for	forty
actor	cord	forgive	forward
dormant	cork	fork	gorse
dormitory	corn	form	gory
dormouse	corner	fort	horn
border	cornflakes	fortnight	
bored	cornflower	fortune	

continued over ☞

B8. Vowel phonemes 'air', 'or', 'er' (continued)

ii. 'or' sound (continued)

or (cont.)

or (cont.)		oor	au
hornet	port		
horse	portable	oor	au
horseshoe	porter	door	astronaut
inspector	porthole	doormat	caught
lord	portion	doorstep	cauldron
matador	portrait	doorway	cause
more	portray	floor	caution
morning	record	indoor	daughter
moron	report	outdoor	haughty
morph	resort		slaughter
morphine	retort	**aw**	
Morse code	sailor	awe	**ore**
morsal	semaphor	claw	adore
mortal	snort	coleslaw	before
mortar	sorcerer	draw	bore
Norway	sore	drawer	chore
nor	sort	fawn	core
normal	sport	flaw	forehead
north	stork	gnaw	ignore
orbit	storm	guffaw	more
orchard	support	hawthorn	ore
orchestra	sword	jackdaw	pore
order	tailor	jaw	score
organ	torch	jigsaw	shore
ordinary	tore	law	snore
organise	torment	lawn	spore
ornament	torn	outlaw	sore
orphan	tornado	paw	store
phosphor	torpedo	pawn	swore
porch	torso	prawn	tore
porcupine	tortoise	raw	wore
pore	torture	saw	
pork	Tory	straw	
porous	tremor	thaw	
porpoise	worn		
	Yorkshire		

iii. 'er' sound

er
advertise
alert
berth
brother
clergy
cloister
confer
convert
desert
dessert
expert
father
farther
former
further
her
herd
hinder
inner
gerbil
knickers

letter
meander
merger
mother
never
over
partner
perhaps
permit
perpetual
perplex
persecute
persevere
persist
person
perspective
perspire
persuade
pervert
prefer
refer
render

reverse
scamper
sermon
serpent
servant
serve
service
sister
stern
tender
term
terminal
terminate

terminus
trainers
transfer
under
verge
vermin
versatile
verse
version
versus
vertebrate
vertival
were

*plus some occupations –
e.g. builder, farmer, footballer,
plumber. etc.*

*plus some nouns based on
verbs – e.g. rider, singer, walker,
finder, sender, leader, lerner, etc.*

*plus comparatives – e.g.
better, nicer, faster, happier, etc.*

ir
affirm
birch
bird
birth
birthday
dirt

fir
firm
gird
girder
girdle
girl
girth

infirmary
ladybird
shirt
sir
skirt
squirt
stir

third
twirl
virgin
virtual
virtue
whirl
whirr

ur
blur
bur
burden
burglar
burn
burp

burst
church
churn
curl
curse
curt
fur

furl
furlong
furnace
furniture
furtive
hurl
hurt

lurch
lurk
murder
murky
nurse
nursery

continued over ☞

B8. Vowel phonemes 'air', 'or', 'er' (continued)

iii. 'er' sound (continued)

ur (cont.)	refurbish	surprise	Turkey
occur	slur	surname	turmoil
purple	spur	survey	turn
purpose	surf	survive	turnip
purr	surface	turban	turpentine
purse	surge	turbine	turquoise
pursue	surgury	turf	
recur	surplus	turkey	

B9. Vowel phonemes 'ear' & 'ea' (taught from Year 2 Term 3)

ear	sear	bread	head
appear	shear	breadth	headteacher
dear	smear	breadwinner	instead
disappear	spear	breakfast	lead
dreary	tear	breast	overhead
ear	year	breaststroke	read
fear		breath	spread
gear	**ea**	breathalyser	thread
hear	ahead	dead	tread
near	blockhead	dread	warhead
rear	bedspread	figurehead	

B10. Other digraphs (taught from Year 2)

ch	cholesterol	chronology	physical
character	choral	chrysalis	physician
chaos	chord		physics
charisma	chorus	**ph**	
chasm	christen	phase	**wh**
chemical	Christianity	phenomenon	whack
chemist	Christmas	philosophy	whale
chemistry	Christopher	phobia	whatever
chlorine	chrome	photocopier	wheat
chlorophyll	chromosome	phoenix	wheel
choir	chronic	photograph	wheelbarrow
cholera	chronicle	phone	wheelchair
		phrase	wheeze

whenever	whip	whisper	wholesale
wherever	whirl	whistle	wholesome
which	whirlpool	white	whoopee
whiff	whirlwind	whoever	why
while	whisk	whole	
whine	whisker	wholemeal	

B11. Multi-syllabic words (taught from Year 2)

adventure	envelope	mathematics
alphabet	family	monopoly
astronaut	fantastic	mountaineer
atishoo	festival	newspaper
basketball	garden	numeracy
bedroom	geography	octopus
biology	gobbledegook	opposite
breakfast	grandfather	playground
budgerigar	grandmother	postman
buttonhole	gymnastics	prehistoric
calculator	handkerchief	pressure
caravan	headteacher	remember
cauliflower	hippopotamus	roundabout
children	history	satellite
chocolate	hospital	Scotland
competition	information	scottish
complicated	intelligent	shopkeeper
computer	interest	supermarket
crocodile	investigate	sweatshirt
cylinder	Ireland	technology
detective	irish	telephone
dictionary	kangaroo	telescope
dinner	ketchup	television
dinosaur	kilogram	tessellate
disappear	kingfisher	umbrella
domino	kitchen	unicorn
dragonfly	ladybird	volcano
elephant	leisure	woodpecker
enchanted	literacy	yesterday
England	lollipop	zodiac
English	marmalade	zoology

Section C. Spelling conventions & rules

C1. Prefixes (taught from Year 3)

anti–
anti-aircraft
antibiotic
anticlimax
anticlockwise
anticyclone
antifreeze
antiseptic

co–
coeducation
coincidence
cooperate
coordinate
correspond

de–
debug
debunk
decipher
decode
decompose
deface
defend
deform
defrost
defuse
dehydrate
demist
denote
depart
deport
depress
derail

dis–
disadvantage
disagree
disappear
disapprove
disconnect
dislike
disloyal
disobey
disrespect
distrust
disused

ex–
exchange
exclaim
exclude
exhale
expand
expel
expire
explain
explore
export
expose
express
exterminate
extract

mis–
misbehave
misfit
misfortune
misjudge
mislay
mislead
misprint
misspell
mistake
mistreat
mistrust
misunderstand
misuse

non–
non-event
non-existent
non-fiction
nonsense
non-stick
non-stop

pre–
precaution
predominate
prefix
prehistoric
prejudge
preoccupied

re–
rearrange
reassure
rebound
rebuild
recall
recapture
reclaim
recoil
recollect
recommend
reconstruct
recover
refill
reform
refresh
refund
regain

remark
remind
remove
renew
repay
replace
replay
reproduce
reread
restore
return
reunion
rewind
rewrite

un–
unable
unavoidable
unaware(s)
unbearable
unbelievable
uncanny
uncertain
uncomfortable
uncommon
unconscious
uncover
undecided
undesirable
undeveloped
undo
undress
unearth
uneasy
unemployed
uneven

unexpected	unhealthy	unnatural	unsuccessful
unfair	unheard-of	unnecessary	unsuitable
unfaithful	unimportant	unoccupied	unthinkable
unfamiliar	uninhabited	unpleasant	untidy
unfashionable	unintentional	unplug	untie
unfasten	unimpressed	unpopular	untrue
unfavourable	uninterested	unreal	unused
unfinished	unjust	unreasonable	unusual
unfit	unkind	unroll	unwanted
unfold	unknown	unscrew	unwell
unforgettable	unleaded	unseen	unwilling
unforgivable	unlikely	unselfish	unwind
unfortunate	unload	unsightly	unwrap
unfriendly	unlock	unskilled	unzip
ungrateful	unlucky	unsound	
unhappy	unmistakable	unsteady	

C2. Suffixes (taught from Year 3)

–ful/fully	successful	briefly	concisely
artful	tearful	brightly	consciously
beautiful	thankful	broadly	daringly
boastful	thoughtful	brokenly	dazzingly
bountiful	useful	busily	dearly
careful	wonderful	cageyly	deathly
cheerful	*plus –ly added to each*	callously	deeply
dreadful	*of the above,*	calmly	dimly
eventful	*e.g. beautifully*	capably	dizzily
faithful		centrally	drearily
frightful	**–ly**	characteristically	famously
fruitful	actively	chattily	fantastically
grateful	alternatively	cheekily	favourably
harmful	amazingly	cheerily	fearlessly
helpful	argumentatively	chiefly	feebly
hopeful	basically	clearly	forcibly
hurtful	bravely	colourlessly	frantically
joyful	brazenly	commonly	friendly
merciful	breathily	compassionately	funnily
respectful	breathlessly	compatibly	
sinful	breezily	competently	continued over ☞

C2. Suffixes (taught from Year 3) (continued)

–ly (continued)

grudgingly	kindly	perfectly	suspiciously
grumpily	knowingly	permanently	technically
happily	loudly	perpetually	terrifically
haltingly	madly	personally	triflingly
handily	mainly	quickly	truly
hardly	markedly	quietly	viciously
haltingly	menacingly	rashly	visually
hazily	merely	seriously	vitally
heavenly	moodily	silently	vividly
hopelessly	namely	slowly	voraciously
humorously	nearly	shortly	weakly
hungrily	newly	splendidly	wickedly
irritatingly	notoriously	suddenly	widely

Most adjectives ending in –y can take the suffix –ly by changing the –y to –i; e.g. jumpy – jumpily. Most adjectives ending in –ic have –al added before the suffix –ly; e.g. mystic – mystically.

C3. Words ending in '–le' (taught from Year 3 Term 1)

able	circle	gaggle	ladle
ample	couple	gentle	mangle
ankle	crackle	giggle	middle
angle	cradle	grapple	mingle
apple	crumble	grumble	meddle
babble	cuddle	gurgle	muddle
battle	cycle	haggle	mumble
bicycle	dabble	handle	needle
boggle	dangle	humble	niggle
bottle	dapple	hurdle	ogle
brittle	dawdle	icicle	paddle
bubble	doddle	idle	possible
bumble	double	invisible	puddle
cable	dribble	jangle	rattle
cackle	fable	jingle	recycle
candle	fickle	juggle	ripple
castle	fiddle	jumble	rumble
cattle	fumble	kindle	rumple

saddle	spittle	toggle	trundle
sample	sprinkle	tickle	tumble
scrabble	squabble	tinkle	turtle
scramble	squiggle	tingle	tussle
scribble	stable	tipple	twiddle
shamble	staple	treacle	twinkle
shackle	startle	treble	uncle
simple	struggle	tremble	vehicle
single	stubble	triangle	visible
snaffle	stumble	trickle	wiggle
spangle	table	tricycle	winkle
sparkle	tackle	trifle	wobble
spectacle	tangle	trouble	wrinkle

plus adjectives formed from nouns and ending in –able, e.g. comfortable, questionable, lovable, etc.

C4. Silent letters (taught from Year 3)

i. silent first letter

gnash	kneel	psalm	wren
gnat	knelt	pseudonym	wrestle
gnaw	knew	psychiatry	wretched
gnome	knife	psychic	wriggle
heir	knight	psychology	wring
honest	knit	whole	wrinkle
honour	knob	wholesale	wrist
hour	knock	wholesome	write
knack	knot	wrap	wrong
knead	knowledge	wreath	
knee	knuckle	wreck	

ii. silent second letter

ghastly	guy	whale	where
ghost	rheumatism	what	whether
ghoul	rhinoceros	wheat	which
guard	rhombus	wheel	whiff
guess	rhubarb	wheelbarrow	while
guest	rhyme	wheelchair	whimper
guide	rhythm	wheeze	
guilty	thyme	when	

continued over ☞

C4. Silent letters (taught from Year 3) (continued)

ii. silent second letter (continued)

whine	whirlwind	whisper	why
whinny	whirr	whistle	
whip	whisk	white	*plus all words*
whirl	whisker	whoopee	*beginning with q–.*

iii. silent endings

bomb	dumb	limb	plumb
comb	jamb	numb	thumb
crumb	lamb	tomb	

C5. Compound words (taught from Year 3)

There are litterally thousands of compund words in the English language. Here is a selection of popular ones.

afternoon	craftsman	flywheel	keyboard
aimless	crossbow	football	know-all
aircraft	crossroads	footbreak	know-how
airmail	crossword	foothold	leakproof
airport	cupboard	footprint	lifebelt
anything	classroom	footnote	lifeboat
anyone	dartboard	goodbye	lifeline
armband	database	greyhound	lifestyle
baseball	daylight	handbag	lifetime
battlefield	deadline	handbreak	lighthouse
birthday	deadlock	handlebars	lunchbox
breakfast	doorway	headteacher	metalwork
become	downstairs	highland(s)	milestone
bedclothes	downtrodden	highlight	milkman
bedroom	everyone	homework	mudguard
bedspread	eyesight	household	needlework
bedtime	fairground	housework	newsagent
beforehand	fireman	however	nightclub
blackberry	fireproof	island	nightdress
bookcase	flowerpot	indoor	nightlight
chairman	flyleaf	internet	nightmare
classroom	flyover	itself	nobleman
cloakroom	flyspray	joyride	noticeboard

overcome	shoelace	sunshine	wallpaper
outlaw	shopkeeper	sunstroke	waterfall
outside	shorthand	timetable	watertight
paintbrush	signpost	tonight	waterproof
passport	skateboard	today	waterworks
peanut	skylight	toyshop	withdraw
playground	skyscraper	turntable	withhold
postcard	snowman	undergo	without
postman	statesman	undergrowth	withstand
pushchair	stockpile	underhand	woodwork
railway	sunbed	underneath	woodworm
rooftop	sunburn	understand	
rucksack	Sunday	undertake(r)	
rainbow	sunlight	underwear	

C6. Two syllable words containing double consonants (taught from Year 4)

bb	cc	ladder	offend
babble	accent	madden	offer
bobbin	accept	middle	offhand
bubble	access	meddle	office
cobble	acclaim	muddle	offside
dabble	accord	nodding	puffin
dribble	account	paddle	puffing
flabby	accuse	pudding	ruffle
grubby	occur	puddle	sniffer
hobble	succeed	ridden	sniffing
hobby	success	sadden	sniffle
jabbed	success	saddle	stiffen
nibble		straddle	stiffly
robber	**dd**	sudden	suffer
rubber	addict	waddle	
shabby	adding	wedding	**gg**
snobbish	bedding		baggage
stabbed	cuddle	**ff**	beggar
stubble	fiddle	gruffly	bigger
stubby	goddess	jiffy	digger
wobble	granddad	muffle	foggy
	hidden	offence	

C6. Two syllable words containing double consonants
(continued)

gg (continued)

gaggle
giggle
haggle
hugging
jogger
juggle
luggage
nugget
ragged
sagged
snigger
snuggle
soggy
stagger
struggle
toggle
wagging
waggle
wiggle

ll
ballet
balloon
ballot
bullet
caller
cellar
collar
collect
college
collide
dollar
duller
fallen
falling
fallow

fellow
filled
gallows
hello
hilly
hollow
holly
jelly
jolly
killer
lolly
lulled
mallet
mellow
miller
milling
mulled
pillow
pollen
pulley
pulling
seller
selling
sullen
swallow
swilling
taller
telling
yelling
yellow

mm
comma
command
comment
commit

committee
common
community
dimmer
drummer
glimmer
hammer
humming
jammed
mammal
mammoth
rammed
stammer
simmer
summer
trimmer

nn
annoy
banner
bonnet
channel
connect
cunning
dinner
funny
gunner
kennel
manner
minnow
nanny
pennant
penny
runner
running
tanner

sinner
sonnet
stunning
thinner
tunnel
winner

pp
appeal
appear
applaud
apple
apply
appoint
approve
chapped
choppy
clapper
clipping
copper
dappled
dipping
flapping
flipper
happy
nappy
pepper
puppy
slapping
slipper
stepping
stipple
supper
tapping
tipper
whopper

rr
arrange
arrest
arrive
arrow
barrel
barrow
berry
borrow
burrow
carrot
carry
correct
curry
flurry
furrow
furry
harrow
horrid
horror
hurry
lorry
marrow
marriage
marry
merry
narrow
parrot
scurry

sorrow
sorry
terror
worry

ss
assess
assist
assume
bassoon
bossy
cassette
fussy
guessing
hassle
hissing
lasso
lesson
massage
message
messy
missing
mossy
passage
passport
password
session
tassel
tossing

tt
attach
attack
attempt
attend
attic
batter
battle
better
bitter
bottle
bottom
butter
button
cattle
cotton
ditto
fatter
fitter
getting
hitting
hotter
jotter
jutting
kettle
kitten
knitting
letter
litter

lotto
matter
mitten
motto
mutter
patter
pattern
potted
putting
quitting
rattle
setter
settle
stutter
tattoo
tatters
tatty
wetting

zz
fizzle
fizzy
fuzzy
grizzly
guzzle
muzzle
sizzle
puzzle

C7. Suffixes (taught from Year 4)

–able
abominable
applicable
collectable
comfortable
controllable
disposable
drinkable
eatable
fashionable
laughable
lovable
questionable
readable
removable
usable
workable
washable

–al
accidental
critical
formal
informal
normal
magical
medical
minimal
mystical
personal
physical
portal

–ary
complimentary
momentary
secondary
stationary

–hood
adulthood
brotherhood
childhood
falsehood
fatherhood
knighthood
motherhood
neighbour-
hood
sisterhood

–ic
artistic
ballistic
cosmic
fantastic
gigantic
futuristic
heroic
historic
meteoric
rustic
scientific

–ible
contemptible
convertible
divisible
edible
incredible
infallible
invisible
legible
sensible
visible

–ive
aggressive

argumentative
attentive
attractive
creative
destructive
excessive
exclusive
expensive
extensive
imaginative
inventive
oppressive
persuasive
preventative
successive
talkative

–ment
achievement
agreement
amazement
amusement
argument
entertain-
ment
fulfilment
settlement
statement

–ness
bitterness
blindness
brightness
calmness
carelessness
cleverness
clumsiness
dampness

eagerness
faithfulness
faithlessness
fondness
fullness
goodness
happiness
hopelessness
kindness
loneliness
meanness
nastiness
neatness
naughtiness
readiness
sadness
sickness
steadiness
sweetness
thankfulness
thoughtfulness
thoughlessness
tidiness
wickedness

–ship
authorship
chairmanship
championship
citizenship
companionship
courtship
dealership
dictatorship
directorship
fellowship
friendship
hardship

headship
ladyship
leadership
lordship
membership
ownership
partnership
premiership
readership
relationship
salesmanship
scholarship
sponsorship
sportsmanship
workmanship

–sion
abrasion
aggression

collision
comprehension
confession
decision
division
erosion
evasion
expansion
explosion
expression
extension
immersion
impression
invasion
invesion
persuasion
precision
suppression
suspension

tension
transfusion

–tion
abolition
action
application
attraction
collection
communication
construction
contraction
creation
destruction
extermination
extinction
extraction
injection
intention

invention
multiplication
notion
perception
potion
prevention
protection
qualification
question
reaction
repetition
solution
subscription
suction
termination
tessellation
transformation
valuation

C8. Common endings (taught from Year 4)

There are very many of these. We present just a selection.

–ight
alight
blight
bright
candlelight
delight
eyesight
fight
flight
fortnight
fright
height
highlight
insight
knight
light
might

night
oversight
right
plight
sight
slight
tight
tonight
twilight
upright
watertight

–tch
batch
bitch
catch
ditch

Dutch
hatch
hitch
latch
match
patch
pitch
snatch
stitch
switch
thatch
watch
witch

–ought
brought
bought

fought
nought
ought
sought
thought
wrought

–aught
caught
fraught
taught

continued over ☞

C8. Common endings (taught from Year 4) (continued)

–ough
although
borough
bough

cough
dough
enough
plough

rough
thorough
through
tough

trough

C10. Vowel endings other than '–e' (Year 5)

–a
Africa
America
Asia
Australia
Austria
camera
Canada
cola
concertina
fantasia
mania
militia
Nigeria
panda

panorama
pasta
pizza
phobia
Russia
Scandinavia
scuba
Tasmania
trivia
tuba
zebra

–i
confetti
okapi

ravioli
timpani
spaghetti

–o
allegro
alto
bamboo
banjo
buffalo
cargo
contralto
echo
halo
hero

largo
mango
piano
potato
shampoo
soprano
tomato
volcano

–u
emu
gnu
Peru
Timbuktu
you

C11. Prefixes (taught from Year 5)

auto–
autobiography
autocrat
autograph
automatic
automobile

circum/circu–
circular
circulate
circumference
circumnavigate
circumstance

in–
inaccurate
inactive
inadequate
incomplete
inconsistent
inconspicuous
incorrect
increase
indefinite
independent
indifferent

inefficient
inexperienced
informal
insecure
insensitive
instead
insufficient
invisible
involuntary

im–
immobile
impassable
impatient

imperfect
impolite
impossible
impractical
imprison
improbable

ir–
irrational
irregular
irrelevant
irresistible
irresponsible

ill–
illegal
illegible
illegitimate
illicit
illiterate
illogical

pro–
proceed
produce
profession
profound

progress
prohibit
project
prolong
prominade
promote
pronoun
propel
propose
protect
protest
protract
protrude

sus–
suspect
suspend
suspense
suspicious
sustain

trans–
transaction
transfer
transform
transfusion
translate

transmit
transport

tele–
telecommu-
   nication
telegraph
telephone
telescope
teletext
television

C12. Suffixes (taught from Year 5)

–ian
beautician
clinician

electrician
magician
mathematician

musician
optician
paediatrician

physician
politician

C13. Prefixes (Year 6)

aer–
aerobatics
aerobics
aeronautics
aeroplane
aerosol

aqu–
aqualung
aquarium
aquatic
aqueduct

au–
audible
audience
audiovisual
audition
auditor
auditorium

auditory

bi–
bicentenary
bicycle
bilingual
binary
binocular
biped
bipolar
bisexual
bivalve

hydr(o)–
hydrant
hydraulic
hydroelectric
hydrofoil
hydrophobia

micro–
microchip
microcosm
microfilm
microphone
microprocessor
microscope
microscopic
microsurgery
microwave

The first edition of *The Teacher's Word Book* was published in 1999. This new edition has been completely revised and enlarged.

Naturally, a short volume like this cannot include every possible word in each of the categories, so we have consulted with teachers to concentrate on words children need and use.

We have had to make some decisions about inclusions and exclusions. In doing this we have been guided by *The Literacy Framework, the Oxford Primary School Dictionary*, and by the suggestions of our advisers.

To keep lists within manageable bounds we have followed a few simple principles.

1. For the most part we have included only root words, not their derivatives. For example, *skill* is listed but not *skilful*.

2. In general we have not included parts of verbs (participles, past tenses and so on). So you will find *sleep* but not *slept*, *creep* but not *crept*, and fall but not *falling*.

3. Except for the list of compound words on page 36 we have included few compounds. The test has been whether the compound word is significantly different in meaning from the originals from which it is formed. However, here as everywhere else decision have sometimes been quite arbitrary.

4. Generally we have omitted slang.

A problem which plagues teachers working on phonemes with speakers of non standard English is regional pronounciation. Most children do not speak 'BBC English' and this hampers some of the phoneme work required by the Framework. For example, in the city near which our company is based, *actor* or *sailor* would be pronounced *actah* and *sailah*! Similar problems are caused by the flatter vowel sounds of English speakers in the north. Accents of children whose roots are in other countries may cause even greater problems. In compiling these lists we have had no choice but to follow received pronounciation. This is a tricky subject, but as experienced English teachers we think it is important for children to be aware of received pronounciation and of the differences between it and the way they themselves speak. *It is vital that this is done without suggesting in any way that the pronounciation of their own culture is inferior. It's just different.*

Of course, many words which possibly could have gone in have been excluded. A useful exercise is to see whether the children in your class can suggest any missing words. One user of the first edition used to hold a competition for children to spot omissions. Although we are always pleased to receive feedback from users, there are no prizes for catching us out!

There are many uses for *The Teacher's Word Book* – spelling lists, word games, quizzes, crosswords, word searches. It is also a deadly resource for Scrabble.

However you use it, we hope you find it helpful.